English Language Learn

Name _____ Date _____

Lesson 11
- ❏ Phonics Word Reading
- ❏ Spelling
- ❏ Sight Words
- ❏ Story 11 ❖ Joseph as a Young Man
- ❏ Vocabulary

Lesson 12
- ❏ Phonics Word Reading
- ❏ Spelling
- ❏ Sight Words
- ❏ Story 12 ❖ Joseph's Rise to Power
- ❏ Vocabulary

Lesson 13
- ❏ Phonics Word Reading
- ❏ Spelling
- ❏ Sight Words
- ❏ Story 13 ❖ Joseph's Family Reunion
- ❏ Vocabulary

Lesson 14
- ❏ Phonics Word Reading
- ❏ Spelling
- ❏ Sight Words
- ❏ Story 14 ❖ The Birth of Moses
- ❏ Vocabulary

Lesson 15
- ❏ Phonics Word Reading
- ❏ Spelling
- ❏ Sight Words
- ❏ Story 15 ❖ The Call of Moses
- ❏ Vocabulary

Lesson 16
- ❏ Phonics Word Reading
- ❏ Spelling
- ❏ Sight Words
- ❏ Story 16 ❖ Ten Plagues and the Passover
- ❏ Vocabulary

Lesson 17
- ❏ Phonics Word Reading
- ❏ Spelling
- ❏ Sight Words
- ❏ Story 17 ❖ The Red Sea
- ❏ Vocabulary

Lesson 18
- ❏ Phonics Word Reading
- ❏ Spelling
- ❏ Sight Words
- ❏ Story 18 ❖ The Ten Commandments
- ❏ Vocabulary

Lesson 19
- ❏ Phonics Word Reading
- ❏ Spelling
- ❏ Sight Words
- ❏ Story 19 ❖ Rahab
- ❏ Vocabulary

Lesson 20
- ❏ Phonics Word Reading
- ❏ Spelling
- ❏ Sight Words
- ❏ Story 20 ❖ Ruth
- ❏ Vocabulary

© Copyright 2017 by John and Jan Walsh ◆ This edition printed August 2019
Published by BibleTelling ◆ 2905 Gill St. ◆ Bloomington, IL 61704, U.S.A. ◆ Cover Design by Joe Horine
To contact the author, email: info@LanguageOlympics.org

Tutor Guide

Overview
- This course is designed for one-on-one tutoring. Anyone who speaks and reads English can serve as a tutor to help an ESL student.
- Each Language Olympics lesson centers around an Old Testament story.
- The Phonics, Sight Words, and Stories in the lessons are available as Audio Assist files on our website, LanguageOlympics.org and in a BibleTelling app. (Instructions at the end of this page)
- Before starting, students are pre-tested. Contact the BibleTelling office for information about the free pretest that goes with this course.

Supplies
- Pencils for all written activities
- Separate paper for spelling practice and test
- Half-sheet of dark paper to help keep student's eyes on each line of text
- Yellow highlighter for marking sight words in the story
- Green pen for tutor signatures
- Bilingual dictionary or electronic translator
- Scripture text in the student's native language

Phonics Word Reading
- This page deals with the sounds of words. It is important for practicing pronunciation.
- Students don't have to know the meanings of all the words on the Phonics page; but if they are curious, look up words using a bi-lingual dictionary or electronic translator. Some students will want to write the word in their language next to each English word.
- Your student may need to hear you say the word first. The tutor reads the word, and the student "echoes". Then the student reads the words alone.

Spelling
- The spelling words are taken from the phonics page. These are selected, based on their frequency of use in everyday language. It is important for the student to know the meaning of the spelling words.
- The student first reads the list of spelling words and then reads each word and spells it aloud.
- Word Meanings: Using a bilingual dictionary or electronic translator, help your student find the meaning of each word in their own language and write it on the line next to the word.
- Finally, the student draws lines to match words with sentences and fills in each blank with the correct English word.
- Spelling (page 2): Match words and pictures.
- Spelling Practice and Test: The tutor dictates the words, and the student writes them. Work on this for a reasonable length of time. If the student is having trouble with certain words, underline them and make a note to review next time.

Sight Words
- Students must learn to instantly recognize the *sight words*. These often don't sound the way they are spelled. Students don't have to spell the sight words — just be able to read them and know the meanings. This prepares learners to read and understand the stories.
- Students will write the meaning of each sight word in their native language.

Use Sight & Spelling Words
The student reads the sentences aloud and matches each one with the best picture. If any of the sentences seem confusing, explain the meanings as needed.

Reading the Story
- Using the Scripture references provided, find the story in the student's native language. You may find the text online and print a copy. The student may also read it on a computer or smartphone – or listen to an audio version.
- Using the list on the left side of the page, the student highlights each word where it appears in the story.
- **Listen to the Story in English:** The tutor reads the story, and the student follows along in the text. OR-the student listens to the story in the Audio Assist files (recordings) on LanguageOlympics.org or in the BibleTelling app.
- The student then reads the entire story aloud with as much help from the tutor as needed.

Story Review and Telling the Story
- The student uses words from the boxes to fill in the blanks.
- Then the student reads the sentences aloud.
- Finally, the student tells the story in his/her own words.

Vocabulary
- The student draws lines to match words and pictures.

Two Options for Listening to Words and Stories

1) Language Olympics website
- Go to LanguageOlympics.org. Look under Tutor and Student Resources. Find English as a Second Language. Click on the green Audio Assists button.
- Choose a lesson and click to hear:
    - Phonics Word Reading
    - Sight Word Reading
    - Story Reading

2) BibleTelling app
- Go to the app store and download the free BibleTelling app. It has a white background and red letters BT.
- Open the app. At the bottom menu bar, select the icon for BibleTelling (two arrows pointing inward).
- Select the light purple ESL box.
- Choose Audio Assists. This takes you to the audio recordings. Choose a lesson and click to hear:
    - Phonics Word Reading
    - Sight Word Reading
    - Story Reading

Lesson 11

Phonics Word Reading

"long o" sounds with oa, ow

When a word has the "long o" sound, you hear the name of the letter o.

☐ Practice reading the phonics words until you have mastered them.

Section 1 — Making the "long o" sound with oa

road	load	loaf	loaves	toad	soak	soaking
oak	oats	coat	goat	boat	coal	goal
foam	soap	oar	roar	board	coach	throat
loan	moan	groan	boast	coast	roast	toast

Section 2 — Making the "long o" sound with ow

mow	mower	crow	row	tow	bow	bow tie
snow	low	glow	slow	flow	blow	below
arrow	fellow	yellow	pillow	follow	hollow	swallow
window	shadow	show	shown	borrow	sorrow	tomorrow
bowl	grow	grown	know	known	throw	thrown

Section 3 — More words with the "long o" sound

oatmeal   road map   toll road

tugboat   lifeboat   houseboat   rowboat

keyboard   pegboard   backboard

☐ My student has mastered the phonics words.   Tutor initials _____

Lesson 11 Spelling (page 1)

"long o" sounds with oa, ow

When a word has the "long o" sound, you hear the name of the letter o.

☐ Read the word list.   ☐ Read each word again and spell it aloud.

below	boat	coat	follow	goal	goat
grow	know	load	low	own	road
row	show	snow	soap	window	yellow

☐ Write the word in your language.   ☐ Draw lines to match the words and sentences.
☐ Use the best English word to fill in the blanks.   ☐ Read the sentences aloud.

below _____   It's cold outside today, so put on your _____.

boat _____   They live in the apartment _____ us.

coat _____   They got into the _____ and crossed the river.

follow _____   Her _____ is to finish reading that book.

goal _____   That _____ ruined our mom's garden.

goat _____   The baby ducks will _____ the mother duck.

grow _____   I _____ how to fix that bike.

know _____   His job was to _____ wood into the wagon.

load _____   Potatoes _____ under the ground.

low _____   She was happy to get a _____ price on food.

own _____   That _____ of beans is dry; it needs water.

row _____   She likes having her _____ bike to ride.

road _____   Will you _____ me how to make a basket?

show _____   We need a _____ map to find our way.

snow _____   The _____ is cold and white.

soap _____   The color of a ripe lemon is _____.

window _____   Use _____ and water to wash your hands.

yellow _____   Do you want this _____ open or closed?

2   ☐ Checked by Tutor   Tutor initials _____

Lesson 11 Spelling (page 2)

"long o" sounds with oa, ow

☐ Read all the words.   ☐ Write the best word under each picture.

boat	coat	goat	pillow	soap	toast
bow	goals	load	road	snow	window

window _____ toast _____ pillow _____ snow _____

bow _____ soap _____ goals _____ goat _____

load _____ road _____ coat _____ boat _____

Spelling Test   ☐ Practice the following words until you have learned them.

1. below   4. follow   7. grow   10. low   13. row   16. soap
2. boat   5. goal   8. know   11. own   14. show   17. window
3. coat   6. goat   9. load   12. road   15. snow   18. yellow

☐ My student can spell these words aloud.   Tutor Initials _____

☐ My student can write these words when I read them.   Tutor Initials _____

Lesson 11 Sight Words

☐ Write the word in your language.
☐ Practice reading the words until you can pronounce them correctly.

belong	blood	bow
charge	color	cry
cried	doing	even
far	field	flock
guard	house	master
money	most	piece
plan	slave	think
throw	twelve	whole

☐ My student can read these words and knows their meanings.   Tutor Initials _____

Lesson 11 – Use Sight & Spelling Words

❏ Read the sentences.   ❏ Draw lines to match the words and pictures.

You can get a whole pie or just one piece.

The slave is following his master.

He's thinking about what to do.

He's throwing some paper into the trash.

He's making a flag with the colors red, yellow, and black.

He always takes a bow at the end of his show.

His job is to carry heavy loads for people.

A guard is watching at the gate.

That man cried the whole night.

They keep their money in a metal box.

It looks like that bowl is full of soup.

She is bowing down to the king.

❏ My student can read and understand these sentences.   Tutor initials _____

Story 11 ◆ Joseph as a Young Man

☐ Read or listen to the story in your native language. Genesis 37:1-36, Genesis 39:1-6

☐ Find and mark the sight words in the story.   ☐ Listen to the story in English.

belong
blood
bow
charge
color
cry
cried
doing
even
far
field
flock
Guard
house
master
money
most
piece
plan
slave
think
throw
twelve
whole

Jacob had twelve sons, but his favorite – the one he loved most – was Joseph, the second-youngest. To show his love, Jacob gave his son a beautiful coat of many colors. Joseph's older brothers were jealous, and they hated him.

Around that time, Joseph had some dreams about his family bowing down to him. When he told his brothers about his dreams, they hated him even more! They didn't want to think about Joseph ruling over them.

One day, Joseph's ten older brothers took their flocks to graze in a field that was far away. Joseph's father sent him to see how his brothers were doing. When the brothers saw Joseph coming, they said, "Here comes that dreamer." Some of them said, "Let's kill him and throw him into a pit. Then we will see what happens to his dreams!"

Reuben (the oldest brother) said, "Don't kill him. Just throw him into a pit." So, they decided to take away his beautiful coat and throw him into a pit. Reuben's plan was to rescue Joseph later and send him home to his father.

After a while, some merchants came by. They were going to Egypt. Suddenly, Judah had an idea. "Let's not kill Joseph. After all, he is our brother. Let's sell him." So they sold him to the merchants for 20 pieces of silver.

Then the brothers killed a goat and dipped Joseph's coat in the blood. When they arrived home, they showed their father the coat and asked, "Does this belong to your son?"

Jacob cried out, "Joseph has been killed by wild animals!" He ripped his clothes and started crying for his son. He said, "I will mourn his death for the rest of my life."

Meanwhile, Joseph was taken to Egypt where he was sold as a slave to Potiphar, Captain of the Guard to the king of Egypt. Joseph worked hard, and God blessed all that he did. His master trusted him and put him in charge of the whole house. He even let Joseph handle the money.

(to be continued)

☐ Read the Story in English.   Tutor initials _____

Review Story 11

☐ Use the words in the boxes to fill in the blanks.

| bowing | colors | even | most | think | twelve |

1. Jacob had _____ sons, but his favorite – the one he loved _____ – was Joseph.
2. To show his love, Jacob gave his son a beautiful coat of many _____.
3. Around that time, Joseph had some dreams about his family _____ down to him.
4. When he told his brothers about his dreams, they hated him _____ more!
5. They didn't want to _____ about Joseph ruling over them.

| belong | blood | doing | far | field | flocks | pieces | plan | throw |

6. One day, Joseph's ten older brothers took their _____ to graze in a _____ that was _____ away.
7. Joseph's father sent him to see how his brothers were _____.
8. Some of Joseph's brothers said, "Let's kill him and _____ him into a pit."
9. Reuben's _____ was to rescue Joseph later and send him home to his father.
10. The brothers sold Joseph to some merchants for 20 _____ of silver.
11. Then the brothers killed a goat and dipped Joseph's coat in the _____.
12. They showed their father the coat and asked, "Does this _____ to your son?"

| charge | cried | crying | Guard | house | master | money | slave | whole |

13. Jacob _____ out, "Joseph has been killed by wild animals!"
14. He ripped his clothes and started _____ for his son.
15. Joseph was taken to Egypt where he was sold as a _____ to Potiphar, Captain of the _____ to the king of Egypt. He worked hard, and God blessed all that he did.
16. Joseph's _____ trusted him and put him in _____ of the _____. _____. He even let Joseph handle the _____.

☐ Read the sentences aloud.   ☐ Tell the story in your own words.   Tutor initials _____

Vocabulary 11 – What are they thinking or saying?

Draw lines to match the words and pictures.

Oh, look at the time! The show will start soon.

I think this is my favorite book!

It is so hot in here!

Oh, no! Not again!

I don't have any bananas. I sold them all!

This belongs on the table with all the other cakes.

I am not going to eat this!

There's no way I can get all this done before 5 o'clock.

I really hope she likes it.

What do you think of my outfit?

This hot drink is going to be good!

I don't know any of these people.

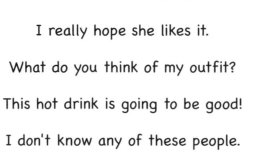

Checked by Tutor   Tutor initials _____

8

Lesson 12
Phonics Word Reading

"long a" sounds with ay & ai

When a word has the "long a" sound, you hear the name of the letter a.

☐ Practice reading the phonics words until you have mastered them.

Section 1 — making the "long a" sound with ay

say	bay	hay	pay	day	today
okay	pray	gray	tray	may	maybe
lay	play	stay	way	away	always

Section 2 — making the "long a" sound with ai

gain	main	pain	rain	train	grain
wait	bait	paid	maid	laid	afraid
aim	air	fair	fairly	sail	sailor
fail	rail	quail	bail	mail	email
jail	nail	tail	hail	pail	paint
daily	pair	chair	stairs	hair	haircut

Section 3 — More words with the "long a" sound

daylight	daytime	weekday	payday	stairway	okay
mailbox	mailman	sailboat	railroad		
airplane	airport	raise	praise		

☐ My student has mastered the phonics words.   Tutor initials _____

Lesson 12 Spelling (page 1)

"long a" sounds with ai & ay

When a word has the "long a" sound, you hear the name of the letter a.

☐ Read the word list.   ☐ Read each word again and spell it aloud.

air	away	daily	day	fair	hair
lay	main	may	paid	pain	pay
rain	sail	say	stay	wait	way

☐ Write the word in your language.   ☐ Draw lines to match the words and sentences.
☐ Use the best English word to fill in the blanks.   ☐ Read the sentences aloud.

air _____   He told the dog to go _____.

away _____   Open the window; I need some fresh _____!

daily _____   Her baby has a _____ bath.

day _____   It's not _____ if he has two and I have only one.

hair _____   She works from nine to five every _____.

fair _____   He wants me to let my _____ grow long.

lay _____   Rice is the _____ thing they like to eat.

main _____   Please _____ your books on the table.

May _____   "_____ God bless you and keep you always!"

paid _____   The old man has a bad _____ in his leg.

say _____   I will get _____ on Friday, and then I can buy food.

pain _____   I won't be long; I just want to _____ goodbye to her.

rain _____   Tomorrow they will _____ their rent.

sail _____   It looks like it will _____ soon.

pay _____   Can you show me how to _____ that little boat?

stay _____   I'm coming; please _____ for me!

wait _____   Do you know the _____ to my house?

way _____   I don't want to go; I want to _____ at home.

☐ Checked by Tutor   Tutor initials _____

Lesson 12 Spelling (page 2)

"long a" sounds with ai & ay

☐ Read all the words.   ☐ Write the best word under each picture.

| hair | mailbox | paint | rail | sailboat | waiter |
| maid | pail | quail | rain | tail | waiting |

_____ _____ _____ _____ _____

_____ _____ _____ _____

_____ _____ _____ _____

Spelling Test ☐ Practice the following words until you have learned them.

1. air	4. day	7. lay	10. paid	13. rain	16. stay
2. away	5. fair	8. main	11. pain	14. sail	17. wait
3. daily	6. hair	9. may	12. pay	15. say	18. way

☐ My student can spell these words aloud.   Tutor Initials _____

☐ My student can write these words when I read them.   Tutor Initials _____

Lesson 12 Sight Words

☐ Write the word in your language.
☐ Practice reading the words until you can pronounce them correctly.

against	always	bought
during	everything	except
grain	great	husband
inside	kept	left
listen	meaning	only
plenty	power	prison
problem	pull	spirit
store	suddenly	tried

☐ My student can read these words and knows their meanings.   Tutor Initials _____

Lesson 12 – Use Sight & Spelling Words

☐ Read the sentences.   ☐ Draw lines to match the words and pictures.

They are painting the house, inside and outside.

His desk is right up against the door.

He's sitting on his bed in the prison.

During supper, he fell asleep on his tray.

There are always plenty of children who will listen to his stories.

A painter is painting a fence post.

That person is inside the tent, except for his feet.

He just left the ice cream store. He bought some for everyone.

Only one person may sit in that chair.

Grain is stored in the silo next to the barn.

Her face shows a spirit of kindness.

The kids are waiting for a ride.

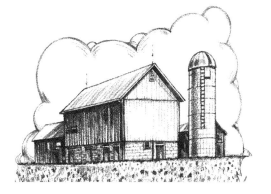

☐ My student can read and understand these sentences.   Tutor initials _____

Story 12 ❖ Joseph's Rise to Power

☐ Read or listen to the story in your native language. Genesis 39, 40, 41, 42:1-5
☐ Find and mark the sight words in the story.   ☐ Listen to the story in English.

against
always
bought
during
everything
except
grain
great
husband
inside
kept
left
listened
meaning
only
plenty
power
prison
problem
pull
spirit
store
suddenly
tried

NOTE
"Famine" is an extreme lack of food

Joseph worked hard as a slave, and his master trusted him. In time, he was in charge of the whole house. But he had a problem with Potiphar's wife. She kept asking Joseph to go to bed with her. Joseph always said, "No! That would be a great sin against God."

One day, when her husband was away, the woman grabbed Joseph when he came inside the house. He tried to get away, but she wouldn't let go. Finally, he left his coat and ran. She was angry! She called her servants and told them that Joseph had come and tried to pull her into bed. She said that he ran away when she screamed. Then she showed them his coat as proof of what she was saying. When her husband came home and heard the story, he had Joseph put into prison.

God was with Joseph and blessed him. In prison, he was given a great job. Soon he was in charge of the whole prison.

One night, Pharaoh, the king of Egypt, had two bad dreams. He needed a wise man to tell him the meaning of his dreams.

Suddenly, someone said, "I know who can help you! His name is Joseph, but he's in prison."

The king sent for Joseph and said to him, "Is it true that you can tell the meaning of dreams?"

Joseph said, "Only God knows the meaning of dreams. He will give you the answer." So the king told him about his two dreams.

Joseph listened, and then he said, "God is showing you what will happen. There will be seven years of great plenty in the land of Egypt. After the seven good years, there will be seven years of famine. You need to store up food during the seven good years, so Egypt will be ready for seven years of famine."

Pharaoh said, "Joseph has the spirit of God in him. No other man is as wise as he is!" Then he said to Joseph, "You are in charge. I want you to store up food for all of Egypt. I'm making you the governor of the land. You will have more power than any man in Egypt, except me."

Everything happened just as God said it would. When the famine came, Joseph sold grain to the people of Egypt. People from other countries also came to Egypt and bought grain from Joseph, the governor. When Joseph's father (Jacob) heard that there was grain in Egypt, he sent his ten older sons to go and buy food; but he kept his youngest son, Benjamin, at home.

(to be continued)

☐ Read the Story in English.   Tutor initials _____

Review Story 12

Use the words in the boxes to fill in the blanks.

| against | always | inside | kept | left | problem | pull | tried |

1. Joseph had a _____ with Potiphar's wife. She _____ asking Joseph to go to bed with her. Joseph _____ said, "No! that would be a great sin _____ God."
2. One day, the woman grabbed Joseph when he came _____ the house.
3. He _____ to get away, but she wouldn't let go. Finally, he _____ his coat and ran. She told everyone that Joseph had tried to _____ her into bed.

| great | husband | listened | meaning | Only | plenty | prison | Suddenly |

4. When her _____ came home, he had Joseph put into _____.
5. There, he was given a _____ job. Soon he was in charge of the whole prison.
6. Pharaoh needed a wise man to tell him the _____ of his dreams.
7. _____, someone said, "I know who can help you!"
8. Joseph said, "_____ God knows the meaning of dreams."
9. Joseph _____, and then he said, "God is showing you what will happen.
10. There will be seven years of great _____ and then seven years of famine."

| bought | during | Everything | except | grain | power | spirit | store |

11. "You need to _____ up food _____ the seven good years, so Egypt will be ready for seven years of famine."
12. Pharaoh said, "Joseph has the _____ of God in him."
13. Then he said to Joseph, "...I'm making you the governor of the land. You will have more _____ than any man in Egypt _____ me."
14. _____ happened just as God said it would. When the famine came, Joseph sold grain to the people in Egypt. People from other countries also came to Egypt and _____ grain from Joseph, the governor.
15. When Joseph's father (Jacob) heard that there was _____ in Egypt, he sent his ten older sons to go and buy food; but he kept his youngest son, Benjamin, at home.

Read the sentences aloud.   Tell the story in your own words.   Tutor initials _____

Vocabulary 12 – What are they thinking or saying?

Draw lines to match the words and pictures.

Please stop crying. It isn't going to help.

I see a problem that needs to be fixed.

I'm training him to say, "Have a great day!"

The guard told me, "Hands up against the wall!"

I know about your problem, and I can help if you will just listen to me.

He tried to pull away, but I kept him close to make sure he was safe.

I'm against this idea, and I have the power to stop it.

I will always be a good husband to you.

I have a great job working on power lines.

I like to pull my wagon to the store.

I'm the only one left in my family.

She is always happy when I hold her this way.

Checked by Tutor   Tutor initials _____

Lesson 13

Phonics Word Reading

Words beginning with bl cl fl gl pl sl

☐ Practice reading the phonics words until you have mastered them.

Section 1 — Words beginning with bl cl fl gl pl sl

| blue | black | block | blank | blame | blaze |
| blow | blew | blown | blood | bless | blessing |

| club | clot | clip | click | close | closed |
| clock | clean | clear | class | clothes | clothing |

| flood | float | flow | flower | flour | floor |
| flag | flat | flax | fly | flew | flown |

| glad | glory | glean | gleam | glow | globe |
| glide | gloves | glass | glasses | glue | gloom |

| plead | please | pleased | plus | place | play |
| plan | plant | plain | plane | plague | plenty |

| slide | sleep | slept | slave | slam | slap |
| slope | slow | slowly | sling | slip | slippery |

Section 2 — More words beginning with bl cl fl pl

blackbird   bluebird   blindfold   blood clot

classroom   clubhouse   clipboard

playground   floorboard   flashlight   flash flood

☐ My student has mastered the phonics words.   Tutor initials _____

Lesson 13 Spelling (page 1)

Words beginning with bl cl fl gl pl sl

☐ Read the word list.   ☐ Read each word again and spell it aloud.

black	blood	class	clean	clear	close
club	flat	flood	floor	fly	glad
place	plan	play	please	sleep	slow

☐ Write the word in your language.   ☐ Draw lines to match the words and sentences.
☐ Use the best English word to fill in the blanks.   ☐ Read the sentences aloud.

black _____   She teaches a _____ of 30 people.
blood _____   He likes to wear mostly _____ and white.
class _____   I cut myself and got _____ on my paper.
clean _____   It is a _____ day—no clouds and no rain.
clear _____   They all like going to boys' _____ after school.
club   _____   I washed my hands, and they are _____.

close _____   I'm so _____ I could help!
flat   _____   Is that land mostly hilly or _____?
flood _____   Don't be afraid! Just stay _____ to me.
fly   _____   He knows how to _____ an airplane.
glad   _____   They had to clean up a huge mess after the _____.
plan   _____   We _____ to go out of town this weekend.

place _____   Both work and _____ are good for children.
play   _____   She needs a _____ to stay until she finds an apartment.
sleep _____   The boys want to _____ outside in a tent.
slow   _____   The girls will sleep inside on the _____.
floor _____   Can you _____ come and help me move?
please _____   She plays _____ music to help her baby sleep.

☐ Checked by Tutor   Tutor initials _____

Lesson 13 Spelling (page 2)

Words beginning with bl cl fl gl pl sl

☐ Read all the words. ☐ Write the best word under each picture.

| blocks | class | flags | glasses | glove | plumber |
| clams | clock | flood | globe | sleep | house plans |

_____

_____

_____

_____

_____

_____

_____

_____

_____

_____

_____

_____

Spelling Test ☐ Practice the following words until you have learned them.

1. black
2. blood
3. class
4. clean
5. clear
6. close
7. club
8. flat
9. flood
10. floor
11. fly
12. glad
13. place
14. plan
15. play
16. please
17. sleep
18. slow

☐ My student can spell these words aloud.   Tutor Initials _____

☐ My student can write these words when I read them.   Tutor Initials _____

Lesson 13 Sight Words

☐ Write the word in your language.
☐ Practice reading the words until you can pronounce them correctly.

become	best	buy
change	city	each
front	full	knew
last	lives	lose
move	need	open
person	prove	short
silver	spies	still
stolen	sure	unless

☐ My student can read these words and knows their meanings.   Tutor Initials _____

Lesson 13 – Use Sight & Spelling Words

❏ Read the sentences.   ❏ Draw lines to match the words and pictures.

One of the spies is looking out the window.

She is buying a silver pin for her mom.

He's running away as if he has stolen something.

It has short legs and long ears.

That animal lives in a tree.

He's using a hand truck to move the barrel.

She likes to play on the slide.

They are in front of their tent.

He's working on a tile floor.

The glass is not all the way full.

He has a puppet on each hand.

He's playing with a puzzle on the floor.

❏ My student can read and understand these sentences.   Tutor initials _____

Story 13 ◆ Joseph's Family Reunion

☐ Read or listen to the story in your native language. Genesis 42, 43, 44, 45
☐ Find and mark the sight words in the story. ☐ Listen to the story in English.

become
best
buy
changed
city
each
front
full
knew
last
lives
lose
move
need
opened
person
prove
short
silver
spies
still
stolen
sure
unless

When the brothers arrived in Egypt, they came before the governor of the land and bowed down. They didn't know it was Joseph. He knew them, but he said, "You are spies!"

They answered, "No, we are good men – all the sons of Jacob who lives in Israel. Our youngest brother is at home, and the other one is gone."

Joseph said, "Prove it to me. I'll keep one of you here in prison. The rest of you go home and get your youngest brother. Don't come back unless he is with you. Then I will believe you." So Joseph kept Simeon in prison.

When the brothers arrived at home they told their father, "We need to take Benjamin to Egypt with us."

Their father said, "No! You are not taking Benjamin away from me. Joseph is gone, and now Simeon is gone. If I lose Benjamin, I will die!"

In time, Jacob told his sons to go back to Egypt and buy more food. But they couldn't go back unless they took Benjamin with them. Judah said to his father, "Let Benjamin go with me. I'll make sure he is safe." At last, Jacob said he could go.

After buying food in Egypt, the brothers started home with their sacks full of grain. Joseph had told his servant to hide a silver cup in Benjamin's sack. When the brothers had gone only a short way, the servants of Joseph ran up and said to them, "One of you has stolen our master's silver cup!"

They answered, "No, we wouldn't do that! If you find that any one of us has it, that person will die, and the rest of us will become slaves to your master."

Each of the brothers opened his sack; there was the cup in Benjamin's sack! The guards took them back to the city. They bowed down in front of Joseph. He asked, "Why have you done this?"

Judah answered, "How can we prove that we didn't do it? All of us will now be your slaves."

"No! Only Benjamin will be my slave. The rest of you can go home."

Judah said, "I promised my father that Benjamin would come home. So I will be your slave. I can't bear to see how sad he will be if the boy doesn't come home."

Then Joseph knew that his brothers had changed. He said, "I am Joseph, the one you sold as a slave." When his brothers heard this, they were afraid.

Joseph said, "Don't be afraid. God sent me here to save your lives. There are still five years of famine left; so go get our father and all your families, and move to Egypt."

When Pharaoh heard that Joseph's family was coming, he said, "The best of Egypt will be theirs!"

Jacob was amazed and happy when his sons told him all that had happened. Then he and his family moved to Egypt. Pharaoh was kind to them there, because of Joseph.

☐ Read the Story in English.   Tutor initials _____

Review Story 13

☐ Use the words in the boxes to fill in the blanks.

| buy | last | lives | lose | need | spies | sure | unless |

1. When Joseph saw his brothers, he knew them, but he said, "You are _____!"
2. They answered, "No, we are good men – all the sons of Jacob who _____ in Israel."
3. Joseph said, "Prove it to me. I'll keep one of you here in prison. The rest of you go home and get your youngest brother. Don't come back _____ he is with you."
4. When the brothers arrived home they told their father, "We _____ to take Benjamin to Egypt with us." Their father said, "No! You are not taking Benjamin away from me. Joseph is gone, and now Simeon is gone. If I _____ Benjamin, I will die!"
5. In time, Jacob told his sons to go back to Egypt and _____ more food. Judah said, "Let Benjamin go with me. I'll make _____ he is safe." At _____, Jacob said he could go.

| become | Each | full | opened | person | short | silver | stolen |

6. The brothers started home with their sacks _____ of grain. Joseph had told his servant to hide a _____ cup in Benjamin's sack. When the brothers had gone only a _____ way, the servants of Joseph ran up and said to them, "One of you has _____ our master's silver cup!"
7. They answered, "No! We wouldn't do that! If you find that any one of us has it, that _____ will die and the rest of us will _____ slaves to your master."
8. _____ of the brothers _____ his sack; there was the cup in Benjamin's sack!

| best | changed | city | front | knew | lives | move | prove | still |

9. The guards took them back to the _____. They bowed down in _____ of Joseph. He asked, "Why have you done this?"
10. Judah answered, "How can we _____ that we didn't do it?"
11. Judah said, "I promised my father that Benjamin would come home. So I will be your slave."
12. Then Joseph _____ that his brothers had _____.
13. Joseph said, "God sent me here to save your _____. There are _____ five years of famine left; so go get our father and all your families, and _____ to Egypt."
14. Pharaoh said, "The _____ of Egypt will be theirs!"

☐ Read the sentences aloud. ☐ Tell the story in your own words. Tutor initials _____

Vocabulary 13 – What are they thinking or saying?

Draw lines to match the words and pictures.

This is hard, and I'm so sleepy!

I'm glad it's lunch time at last!

This jar is easy to close but hard to open.

Say it slowly; I need to be sure
I hear each word right.

Stay with me. I don't want to lose you!

I'm going to need a tall ladder for this job.

I'm glad you called.
I need to talk to you about this plan.

There's no way I can use that bike unless
I get the flat tire fixed.

Wow! This desk is clean!

I'm feeling sad. I really miss my best friend
since she moved away.

They sure are taking a long time! I'm
getting tired of waiting.

I knew I could get 100%, and I did!

☐ Checked by Tutor   Tutor initials _____

Lesson 14

Phonics Word Reading

Words beginning with br cr dr fr gr pr tr

☐ Practice reading the phonics words until you have mastered them.

Section 1 — Words beginning with br cr dr fr gr pr tr

| bread | brag | brass | bring | brought | brave | brakes |
| brick | brown | bride | brother | break | broke | broken |

| cry | cried | cries | crash | crafts | crack | crackers |
| crop | crowd | crime | crazy | cruel | cross | crossing |

| draw | drew | drag | dress | drill | drip | dripping |
| drop | drug | drive | drove | dream | drink | drank |

| frame | friend | from | front | free | freeze | freedom |
| fresh | frown | fry | fried | fries | fright | fraction |

| grand | grain | grow | grown | grew | group | ground |
| green | greet | grave | grade | great | grace | grass |

| prison | prove | proof | pretty | price | problem | provide |
| prize | pride | proud | print | praise | pray | prayer |

tree	trunk	tribe	try	tried	tries	trial
track	trust	truck	train	training	trade	trail
true	trick	trip	trash	travel	traffic	trouble

Section 2 — More words beginning with br dr fr gr

bricklayer   daybreak   driveway   friendship

grandmother   grandfather   grandchildren   grasshopper   greenhouse

☐ My student has mastered the phonics words.   Tutor initials _____

Lesson 14 Spelling (page 1)
Words beginning with br cr dr fr gr pr tr

☐ Read the word list.   ☐ Read each word again and spell it aloud.

bread	break	crop	cry	cried	drive
drink	friend	from	front	grass	great
green	group	pretty	trip	try	tried

☐ Write the word in your language.   ☐ Draw lines to match the words and sentences.
☐ Use the best English word to fill in the blanks.   ☐ Read the sentences aloud.

bread _____   If you drop that glass bowl, it will _____.
break _____   We need to get some _____ so we can make toast.
crop _____   The hot sand on her feet made her _____ out in pain.
cry _____   We had a good _____ of potatoes this year.
drink _____   When he was 16, he learned to _____ a jeep.
drive _____   Would you like a _____ of cold water?

---

cried _____   He is from India. Where are you _____?
friend _____   When she lost her money, she just sat and _____.
from _____   You are my very best _____.
front _____   Grandpa was always glad to mow the _____ for us.
grass _____   She has a _____ love for her students.
great _____   Do you want to sit in the _____ or the back?

---

green _____   She is a very _____ girl.
group _____   After a long rain, all the grass will be _____.
pretty _____   If we have ten people, we can get a _____ rate.
trip _____   I don't think I can swim, but I will _____.
try _____   I _____ to call two times, but there was no answer.
tried _____   It is a long _____ between London and New York.

☐ Checked by Tutor   Tutor initials _____

Lesson 14 Spelling (page 2)

Words beginning with br cr dr fr gr pr tr

☐ Read all the words.   ☐ Write the best word under each picture.

| bread | bride | drapes | drill | frog | tree |
| bricks | crab | dress | drum | grapes | truck |

Spelling Test ☐ Practice the following words until you have learned them.

1. bread	4. cry	7. drink	10. front	13. green	16. trip
2. break	5. cried	8. friend	11. grass	14. group	17. try
3. crop	6. drive	9. from	12. great	15. pretty	18. tried

☐ My student can spell these words aloud.   Tutor Initials _____

☐ My student can write these words when I read them.   Tutor Initials _____

Lesson 14 Sight Words

☐ Write the word in your language.
☐ Practice reading the words until you can pronounce them correctly.

another	birth	born
brought	child	close
different	edge	felt
fight	finally	girl
grew	king	large
must	new	number
own	river	sister
something	strong	war

☐ My student can read these words and knows their meanings.   Tutor Initials _____

Lesson 14 – Use Sight & Spelling Words

☐ Read the sentences.   ☐ Draw lines to match the words and pictures.

A baby is in a basket close to the edge of the river.

They are using a large number of bricks to make a huge wall.

Each person brought something for the birth of a new child.

He's trying to become strong.

Their new baby may have been born last week.

He is glad to stay close to his big sister.

She wants that cat to get off the edge of her dress.

She's glad to have her own desk.

They are going to fight in a war.

He wants the little plant to grow.

His plant grew taller than he is.

They have a new crib for their baby.

☐ My student can read and understand these sentences.   Tutor initials _____

Story 14 ◆ The Birth of Moses

☐ Read or listen to the story in your native language. Exodus 1, Exodus 2:1-10

☐ Find and mark the sight words in the story.   ☐ Listen to the story in English.

Sight Words
another
birth
born
brought
child
close
different
edge
felt
fight
finally
girl
grew
king
large
must
new
number
own
river
sister
something
strong
war

NOTE
A "midwife" helps women with childbirth.

Jacob brought 70 people with him when he moved his family to Egypt. They were called Hebrews or Israelites. In time, Jacob and all of his sons died. Their descendants did well in Egypt, and their population grew very large.

Then a new king (Pharaoh) came to power in Egypt. He didn't know about Joseph and all that he had done to help Egypt. The king did not like having so many Israelites in his country. He was afraid that, in a time of war, the Israelites might fight against Egypt. So Pharaoh made all the Israelites become slaves of the Egyptians. They had to work hard making bricks and building cities. The bosses were cruel to the slaves, but still their numbers grew very large.

Then Pharaoh thought of another plan. He called in all the Hebrew midwives and told them, "When you help an Israelite woman have her child, kill all baby boys as soon as they are born. You may let the baby girls live."

The midwives feared God and did not obey Pharaoh. They let all the baby boys and the baby girls live. God blessed the midwives because they did not kill the baby boys. The Israelites kept growing in number, and they were very strong.

Then Pharaoh came up with a new plan. He said, "Every Israelite baby boy must be thrown into the Nile River."

During this time, a boy was born into one of the Israelite families. For three months after his birth, his mother hid him. But, as he grew, it was harder to keep him hidden.

Finally, she knew she had to do something different. The mother made a waterproof basket, placed the child inside, and put the basket in the reeds close to the edge of the river. The boy's sister hid nearby so she could see what would happen to her baby brother.

When Pharaoh's daughter came down to the river to take a bath, she found the basket floating in the river. When she opened it, the baby started to cry, and she felt sorry for it. She said, "This must be one of the Israelite children." She wanted to keep the baby.

The boy's sister came out of her hiding place and asked. "Do you want me to go and find an Israelite mother to nurse this child?"

Pharaoh's daughter looked at her and said, "Yes, I'd like that! Go find a nursing mother." So, the girl went and got her own mother, the mother of the child. Pharaoh's daughter said to her, "Nurse this child for me and I will pay you." So, the child's mother was paid to be his nurse.

When the boy was old enough, his mother brought him back to Pharaoh's daughter, and he became her son. She called him Moses, meaning 'pulled out' because, she said, "I pulled him out of the water."

☐ Read the Story in English.   Tutor initials _____

Review Story 14

☐ Use the words in the boxes to fill in the blanks.

| another | fight | girls | king | large | number | strong | war |

1. A new _____ (Pharaoh) came to power in Egypt. He didn't know about Joseph.
2. He was afraid that, in a time of _____, the Israelites might _____ against Egypt.
3. So Pharaoh made all the Israelites become slaves of the Egyptians. The bosses were cruel to the slaves, but still their numbers grew very _____.
4. Then Pharaoh thought of _____ plan. He told the midwives to kill all baby boys as soon as they were born. But the midwives let all the baby boys and the baby _____ live.
5. The Israelites kept growing in _____, and they were very _____.

| birth | born | new | Finally | grew | must | something | different |

6. Then Pharaoh came up with a _____ plan. He said, "Every Israelite baby boy _____ be thrown into the Nile River."
7. During this time, a boy was _____ into one of the Israelite families. For three months after his _____, his mother hid him. But as he _____, it was harder to keep him hidden.
8. _____, she knew she had to do _____ _____.

| brought | child | close | edge | felt | own | river | sister |

9. The mother made a waterproof basket, placed the child inside, and put the basket in the reeds _____ to the _____ of the river. The boy's _____ hid nearby.
10. When Pharaoh's daughter came down to the _____ to take a bath, she found the basket floating in the river. When she opened it, the baby started to cry, and she _____ sorry for it. The boy's sister came out of her hiding place and asked, "Do you want me to go and find an Israelite mother to nurse this _____?"
11. The girl went and got her _____ mother, the mother of the child.
12. When the boy was old enough, his mother _____ him back to Pharaoh's daughter, and he became her son.

☐ Read the sentences aloud.   ☐ Tell the story in your own words.   Tutor initials _____

31

Vocabulary 14 – What are they thinking or saying?

Draw lines to match the words and pictures.

No, I'm not working; I'm taking a break.

Is there something you want to ask me?

I'm looking for something. It must be in here!

Here, I brought you another piece of bread.

They didn't know I was her mom; they thought I was her sister!

Would you like something to eat?

I'm freezing cold. I need another drink of something hot.

I'm strong. I will fight with anyone!

Something is wrong with this watermelon!

My baby is finally asleep!

Don't you feel even a little bit sorry for me?

I tried to help, but it didn't work. I must think of another way.

Checked by Tutor   Tutor initials _____

Lesson 15
Phonics Word Reading
Words beginning with sk sm sn sw sp st

☐ Practice reading the phonics words until you have mastered them.

Section 1 ~ Words beginning with sk sm sn sw sp st

sky	skate	skill	skull	skid	skip	skin
small	smile	smell	smoke	smack	smart	smooth
snail	snow	snap	snack	snake	sneak	sneeze

| sway | swing | swipe | sweep | sweet | swim | swimming |
| switch | swarm | swear | sweat | swap | swamp | swallow |

spin	spit	split	spirit	spell	spot	space
speed	speech	speak	spoke	spare	spear	spread
spy	spies	spider	spring	spoon	spend	spent

stab	step	stick	stuck	stuff	study	student
stack	staff	stand	stood	still	stop	stocking
steal	stole	stolen	stone	storm	store	story
steel	steer	star	start	stairs	state	stay
street	stream	strike	stroke	strong	stress	stray

Section 2 ~ More words beginning with sk sw sp st

sweater   sweatshirt   swimsuit   sweetheart

stepladder   stoplight   stairway   strawberry   storytelling

skateboard   spokesman   sports   speed limit   bus stop

☐ My student has mastered the phonics words.   Tutor initials _____

Lesson 15 Spelling (page 1)

Words beginning with sk sm sn sw sp st

☐ Read the word list.   ☐ Read each word again and spell it aloud.

skin	small	smell	speak	spoke	speed
staff	stand	stood	state	step	still
stone	stop	street	strong	study	student

☐ Write the word in your language.   ☐ Draw lines to match the words and sentences.
☐ Use the best English word to fill in the blanks.   ☐ Read the sentences aloud.

skin _____   Do you _____ smoke?
small _____   Her _____ is red after being in the sun.
smell _____   Do you want the _____ or large size?
speak _____   She can _____ English and two more languages.
spoke _____   We must always drive at a safe _____.
speed _____   Last night he _____ for 40 minutes.

staff _____   You should _____ and let your mom sit down.
stand _____   How many people are on your office _____?
stood _____   She lives in the _____ of Texas.
state _____   He _____ out in the rain and waited for me.
still _____   Along the river, I found a flat, round _____.
stone _____   It was a _____ night; there was no wind at all.

stop _____   The old woman is not _____; she is weak.
street _____   When the light is red, we have to _____.
strong _____   Our friends live across the _____ from us.
step _____   She will _____ so she can pass her driving test.
study _____   That _____ works hard to get good grades.
student _____ Be careful not to _____ in the puddle of water.

☐ Checked by Tutor   Tutor initials _____

Lesson 15 Spelling (page 2)

Words beginning with sk sm sn sw sp st

☐ Read all the words.   ☐ Write the best word under each picture.

| snail | snowman | star | study | swim | skate |
| snake | stairs | store | swan | swings | skateboard |

Spelling Test   ☐ Practice the following words until you have learned them.

1. skin	4. speak	7. staff	10. state	13. stone	16. strong
2. small	5. spoke	8. stand	11. step	14. stop	17. study
3. smell	6. speed	9. stood	12. still	15. street	18. student

☐ My student can spell these words aloud.   Tutor Initials _____

☐ My student can write these words when I read them.   Tutor Initials _____

Lesson 15 Sight Words

☐ Write the word in your language.
☐ Practice reading the words until you can pronounce them correctly.

able	being	burn
care	else	forty
lead	mouth	never
palace	prepare	send
shepherd	shoes	slow
someone	strike	suffer
teach	therefore	trouble
won't	worship	yet

☐ My student can read these words and knows their meanings.   Tutor Initials _____

Lesson 15 – Use Sight & Spelling Words

❑ Read the sentences.   ❑ Draw lines to match the words and pictures.

He is able to walk, but he can't walk by himself yet.

They are having a staff meeting to prepare a report.

He's still suffering great pain with his broken arm.

He is preparing to strike the wood with his ax.

He is not strong, therefore she takes care of him.

That small dog with spots is not mine; it belongs to someone else.

That bush is burning, and yet, it is not being burned up.

He will walk slowly as he leads his horse.

That shepherd has only two sheep with him.

He was slow to start work, and now he's in trouble.

The shepherd's staff is in his right hand.

The old stone palace is still standing.

❑ My student can read and understand these sentences.   Tutor initials _____

Story 15 ❖ The Call of Moses

☐ Read or listen to the story in your native language. Ex. 2:11-25, Ex. 3:1-22, Ex. 4:1-18
☐ Find and mark the sight words in the story.   ☐ Listen to the story in English.

able
being
burn
cared
else
forty
lead
mouth
never
palace
prepared
send
shepherd
shoes
slow
someone
strike
suffer
teach
therefore
trouble
won't
worship
yet

Moses grew up in the palace of the king of Egypt. Still, he cared about his people, the Israelites. One day, when Moses was 40 years old, he saw an Israelite and an Egyptian fighting. He tried to help the Israelite by killing the Egyptian, but someone saw him. He was in trouble, so he ran away to the land of Midian. There he married a young woman and worked as a shepherd for his father-in-law.

Forty years later, (when Moses was 80 years old) the Israelites were still slaves in Egypt. God wanted to use Moses to bring his people to freedom.

One day, Moses was out taking care of his flock near Mt. Sinai. Suddenly, he saw a fire burning in a bush, yet the bush was not being burned up. As Moses came close to the bush, God called to him, "Stop! Take off your shoes; you are standing on holy ground. I am the God of your fathers – the God of Abraham, Isaac, and Jacob."

God said, "My people are suffering greatly in Egypt. I am sending you there to get them and lead them back to the land of Canaan. Go tell Pharaoh to let my people go."

Moses said, "Oh, Lord, not me! I'm not able to talk to Pharaoh, and I'm not able to lead the Israelites out of Egypt."

God said, "I will be with you. Go to Egypt and bring my people back here to worship. The people will listen to you, but Pharaoh won't. Therefore, I will strike him hard, until he finally lets my people go."

Moses said, "Lord, I've never been able to talk well. I have trouble talking, and my speech is very slow."

God asked, "Moses, who made your mouth? I am the one who makes a person to be deaf, mute, blind, or seeing! Go, and do as I say. I will help you talk, and I will teach you what to say."

Moses answered, "I just don't want to go. Please send someone else."

Then the Lord became angry. "Your brother Aaron is coming to meet you. He will be your spokesman. Take him and go to Egypt as I have told you." Finally, Moses agreed, and he prepared to go to Egypt.

☐ Read the Story in English.   Tutor initials _____

Review Story 15

☐ Use the words in the boxes to fill in the blanks.

| being | burning | cared | Forty | palace | shepherd | trouble | yet |

1. Moses grew up in the _____. Still, he _____ about his people, the Israelites.
2. He was in _____, so he ran away to the land of Midian. There he married a young woman and worked as a _____ for his father-in-law.
3. _____ years later, (when Moses was 80 years old) the Israelites were still slaves in Egypt.
4. Moses saw a fire _____ in a bush, _____ the bush was not _____ burned up.

| able | lead | sending | shoes | strike | suffering | Therefore | won't | worship |

5. As Moses came close to the bush, God called to him, "Stop! Take off your _____; you are standing on holy ground."
6. God said, "My people are _____ greatly in Egypt. I am _____ you there to get them and _____ them back to the land of Canaan. Go tell Pharaoh to let my people go."
7. Moses said, "Oh, Lord, not me! I'm not _____ to talk to Pharaoh."
8. God said, "I will be with you. Go to Egypt and bring my people back here to _____. The people will listen to you, but Pharaoh _____."
9. _____, I will _____ him hard until he finally lets my people go."

| else | mouth | never | prepared | slow | someone | teach |

10. Moses said, "Lord, I've _____ been able to talk well. I have trouble talking, and my speech is very _____."
11. God asked, "Moses, who made your _____? I will help you talk, and I will _____ you what to say."
12. Moses answered, "I just don't want to go. Please send _____ _____."
13. Finally, Moses agreed, and he _____ to go to Egypt.

☐ Read the sentences aloud.   ☐ Tell the story in your own words.   Tutor initials _____

Vocabulary 15 – What are they thinking or saying?

Draw lines to match the words and pictures.

I'm trying to show that I care about you.

I wish I had someone to play ball with me.

We can't get anyone else on this swing.

No one cares how I feel.

This is not a club in my hand; it's my walking stick.

Help! There's trouble here and I'm not able to take care of it.

If someone will teach me, I know I am able to do this.

Even if I am forty, I still like to hug my dad.

Mmm...Those pies smell so good!

I think I see someone I know!

I don't care what you think; I will do as I please!

Now, listen to me – I'm the boss, and I won't put up with a slow worker!

Lesson 16
Phonics Word Reading
Words ending in sk & st

☐ Practice reading the phonics words until you have mastered them.

Section 1 — Words ending in sk

| desk | ask | cask | mask | task | flask |
| dusk | husk | tusk | disk | risk | brisk |

Section 2 — Words ending with the st sound

fast	mast	past	vast	cast	last	best
nest	test	vest	west	rest	arrest	against
guest	list	mist	first	post	most	almost
dust	just	must	gust	rust	crust	trust
August	locust	east	beast	feast	least	yeast
taste	paste	haste	waste	roast	coast	toast
lost	cost	frost	chest	quest	request	suggest

Section 3 — More words ending with st

harvest   forest   honest   breakfast   forecast

motorist   cyclist   artist   dentist   florist   tourist   scientist

☐ My student has mastered the phonics words.   Tutor initials _____

Lesson 16 Spelling (page 1)
Words ending in sk & st

☐ Read the word list.   ☐ Read each word again and spell it aloud.

almost	best	cost	desk	east	fast
first	just	last	list	lost	must
nest	past	rest	test	trust	west

☐ Write the word in your language.   ☐ Draw lines to match the words and sentences.
☐ Use the best English word to fill in the blanks.   ☐ Read the sentences aloud.

almost _____   My _____ time to study is in the morning.
best   _____   I'm _____ ready to go.
cost   _____   New York is on the _____ coast of the US.
desk   _____   How much does it _____ to get a phone?
east   _____   Please don't talk so _____!
fast   _____   She keeps paper and pencils in her _____.

nest _____   I need to go home and _____.
just _____   Three baby birds are in that _____.
last _____   She always takes a shopping _____ with her.
list _____   We _____ moved into our apartment yesterday.
rest _____   If you want to pass the test, you _____ study.
must _____   The cookies are gone; I ate the _____ one.

first _____   He _____ his glasses, but then he found them.
past _____   That boy always wants to be _____ in line.
lost _____   Are you ready for your driving _____?
test _____   In the _____, she always came on time.
trust _____   California is on the _____ coast of the US.
west _____   I _____ you to take care of my plants.

☐ Checked by Tutor   Tutor initials _____

Lesson 16 Spelling (page 2)

Words ending in sk & st

☐ Read all the words.   ☐ Write the best word under each picture.

| artist | desk | vest | husk | nest | tusk |
| dentist | mask | forest | list | rest | first place |

_____   _____   _____   _____

_____   _____   _____   _____

_____   _____   _____   _____

Spelling Test ☐ Practice the following words until you have learned them.

1. almost	4. desk	7. first	10. list	13. nest	16. test
2. best	5. east	8. just	11. lost	14. past	17. trust
3. cost	6. fast	9. last	12. must	15. rest	18. west

☐ My student can spell these words aloud.   Tutor Initials _____

☐ My student can write these words when I read them.   Tutor Initials _____

Lesson 16 Sight Words

☐ Write the word in your language.
☐ Practice reading the words until you can pronounce them correctly.

absolutely	cause	cover
darkness	door	ever
everywhere	face	flies
frog	green	leave
mark	message	mind
order	pass	perfect
plant	sorry	storm
today	tomorrow	turn

☐ My student can read these words and knows their meanings.   Tutor Initials _____

Lesson 16 – Use Sight & Spelling Words

❑ Read the sentences.   ❑ Draw lines to match the words and pictures.

He does <u>not</u> want us to go fast.

She always does a 'taste test' before serving the rest of her family.

He just got that cast on his leg today.

He's glad he's getting his cast off tomorrow.

Her desk is in perfect order.

He's almost all the way under the covers.

He is face to face with his dog.

He has his best rest when he uses his hat to cover his face.

He needs his cane in order to walk.

Green plants have come up in all the fields

She is just turning on the stove.

She's waiting for her turn to use the well.

❑ My student can read and understand these sentences.   Tutor initials _____

45

Story 16 ❖ Ten Plagues and the Passover

☐ Read or listen to the story in your native language.

Ex.5:1-19, Ex.6:1-13, Ex.7:1-25, Ex.8:1-32, Ex.9:1-35, Ex.10:1-29, Ex.11:1-10, Ex.12:1-42

☐ Find and mark the sight words in the story.   ☐ Listen to the story in English.

Sight Words
absolutely
cause
cover
darkness
door
ever
everywhere
face
flies
frogs
green
leave
mark
message
mind
ordered
pass
perfect
plant
sorry
storm
today
tomorrow
turn

NOTE
"Plagues" were troubles sent by God as punishment.

Moses and Aaron went to Pharaoh, the king of Egypt, and asked him to let the Israelites go into the desert and worship. Pharaoh answered, "No, absolutely not!"

Moses said to Pharaoh, "Because you will not let our people go, the water in the river will turn into blood." That was the first plague. Soon all the water in Egypt was blood. The people had to dig wells to find good water.

After seven days, Moses told Pharaoh, "Because you will not let our people go, frogs will be everywhere on your land." Soon, frogs started coming out of the river. They went into people's houses, into their food, and into their beds! Pharaoh asked Moses to get rid of the frogs, and he promised to let the people go. The next day the frogs died, but Pharaoh changed his mind and wouldn't let the people go. Next, God sent lice on all the people and animals in Egypt.

After that, God sent swarms of flies to cover the land, and Pharaoh said the people could leave. But the next day, when the flies were gone, Pharaoh changed his mind again. Then God caused all of Egypt's cattle to die, but Pharaoh still wouldn't let the people go. God also sent boils on the Egyptians and their animals.

Moses went to Pharaoh with another message from God: "Tomorrow I'll send hail like you've never seen before!" When the storm came, Pharaoh begged Moses to make it stop. But, as soon as it did stop, he changed his mind again.

After that, locusts came and ate every green plant on the land. Pharaoh said, "I'm sorry for my sin. Please ask God to take the locusts away." But when the locusts were gone, he still wouldn't let the people go.

Next, God sent darkness over the land for three days. Pharaoh said, "Your people may go and worship, but leave your animals here."

Moses answered, "Absolutely not!" We will take everyone and everything – even the animals."

Then Pharaoh was angry! "Get away from me, and don't ever come back! Mark my word – you will die if you ever see my face again!"

The Lord told Moses, "I will bring one last plague on the Egyptians, and then Pharaoh will let the people go. Tell my people this: 'Every family must take a perfect male lamb, kill it, and put its blood on the door posts and above the door. Then the family must stay inside their home.

At midnight I will pass over all the land of Egypt and kill the firstborn in every home; but when I see the blood on your houses, I will pass over you.'"

Everything happened just as God said. Then Pharaoh ordered, "Go! Take your people and your flocks, and leave!" So the people left while it was still night. After that, the Israelites celebrated Passover every year; and they still do today.

☐ Read the Story in English.   Tutor initials _____

Review Story 16

❑ Use the words in the boxes to fill in the blanks.

| caused | cover | everywhere | flies | frogs | mind | turn |

1. "Because you will not let our people go, the water in the river will _____ into blood."
2. "Because you will not let our people go, frogs will be _____ on your land."
3. Pharaoh asked Moses to get rid of the _____, and he promised to let the people go.
4. The next day the frogs died, but Pharaoh changed his _____ and wouldn't let the people go.
5. After that, God sent swarms of _____ to _____ the land, Pharaoh said the people could leave. But when the flies were gone, Pharaoh changed his mind again.
6. Then God _____ all of Egypt's cattle to die.

| darkness | green | message | plant | sorry | storm | Tomorrow |

7. Moses went to Pharaoh with another _____ from God; "_____ I'll send hail like you've never seen before!"
8. When the _____ came, Pharaoh begged Moses to make it stop. But, as soon as it did stop, he changed his mind again.
9. After that, locusts came and ate every _____ _____ on the land.
10. Pharaoh said, "I'm _____ for my sin" But he still wouldn't let the people go.
11. Next, God sent _____ over the land for three days.

| Absolutely | door | ever | face | leave | Mark | ordered | pass | perfect | today |

12. Pharaoh said to Moses, "Your people may go and worship, but _____ your animals here."
13. Moses answered, "_____ not! We will take everyone and everything - even the animals."
14. Then Pharaoh was angry! "Get away from me, and don't _____ come back!
15. _____ my word – you will die if you ever see my _____ again!"
16. The Lord told Moses, "Every family must take a _____ male lamb, kill it, and put its blood on the door posts and above the _____. Then the family must stay inside their home.
17. At midnight I will pass over all the land of Egypt and kill the firstborn in every home; but when I see the blood on your houses, I will _____ over you."
18. Everything happened just as God said. Then Pharaoh _____, "Go! Take your people and your flocks, and leave!" So the people left while it was still night.
19. After that, the Israelites celebrated Passover every year; and they still do _____.

❑ Read the sentences aloud.   ❑ Tell the story in your own words.   Tutor initials _____

Vocabulary 16 – What are they thinking or saying?

Draw lines to match the words and pictures.

Just fix this one thing and we will be ready for tomorrow's meeting.

That was your best job ever!

It's not possible to get these bricks lined up perfectly.

I'm so sorry, I've got to get off the phone.

This soup is perfect!

Thank you for writing on my cast.

This desk is the perfect place for me to rest.

We can leave now through this door.

I don't mind if my dog licks my face.

I did not get what I ordered.

It was good meeting you. See you tomorrow.

Mark my word. If you don't listen to me, you will be sorry!

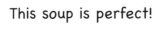

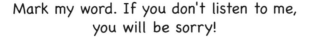

☐ Checked by Tutor   Tutor initials _____

Lesson 17
Phonics Word Reading
Words containing ft ld lp lt mp nd nt pt

☐ Practice reading the phonics words until you have mastered them.

Section 1 — words containing nd

and	band	grand	hand	handle	land	island
sand	stand	wind	windy	window	end	bend
mend	lend	tend	attend	pretend	send	spend
defend	depend	friend	second	beyond	pond	under
fund	refund	find	kind	mind	remind	behind

Section 2 — words containing nt

ant	pant	plant	hunt	want	rent	tent
went	sent	spent	meant	parent	front	different
hint	print	absent	repent	bent	dent	dental

Section 3 — words containing ft lt mp pt lp ld

gift	lift	left	soft	raft	craft	draft
belt	felt	melt	wilt	tilt	quilt	built
bolt	colt	jolt	salt	halt	adult	result
damp	lamp	ramp	camp	cramp	clamp	stamp
stump	jump	dump	lump	pump	bump	hump
empty	kept	help	held	hold	bald	world

☐ My student has mastered the phonics words.   Tutor initials _____

Lesson 17 Spelling (page 1)

Words containing ft ld lp lt mp nd nt pt

☐ Read the word list.   ☐ Read each word again and spell it aloud.

felt	find	hand	kept	kind	land
left	meant	mind	parent	result	second
send	sent	spend	want	went	wind

☐ Write the word in your language.   ☐ Draw lines to match the words and sentences.
☐ Use the best English word to fill in the blanks.   ☐ Read the sentences aloud.

felt _____   He's trying to _____ his keys!
find _____   Please _____ me a paper towel.
hand _____   Yesterday I _____ fine, but today I'm sick.
kept _____   That _____ is good for farming.
kind _____   As a child, she always _____ her room clean.
land _____   What _____ of bread do you like best?

---

left _____   I _____ to call you last night, but I forgot.
meant _____   They _____ home at 7:00 this morning.
mind _____   Do you _____ if I sit here?
parent _____   That fallen tree is a _____ of yesterday's storm.
result _____   Their first child was a boy, and their _____ was a girl.
second _____   She wants to be a good _____.

---

send _____   Do you _____ some help?
sent _____   Last week, I _____ her a birthday card.
want _____   I hope she will _____ me a letter this week.
spend _____   The whole family _____ on a picnic together.
went _____   A strong _____ made huge waves on the lake.
wind _____   How much did you _____ for food last month?

☐ Checked by Tutor   Tutor initials _____

Lesson 17 Spelling (page 2)

Words containing ft ld lp lt mp nd nt pt

☐ Read all the words.   ☐ Write the best word under each picture.

| ants | belt | gift | jump | pants | second |
| band | tent | hand | lamp | plant | camping |

Spelling Test   ☐ Practice the following words until you have learned them.

1. felt
2. find
3. hand
4. kept
5. kind
6. land
7. left
8. meant
9. mind
10. parent
11. result
12. second
13. send
14. sent
15. spend
16. want
17. went
18. wind

☐ My student can spell these words aloud.   Tutor Initials _____

☐ My student can write these words when I read them.   Tutor Initials _____

Lesson 17 Sight Words

☐ Write the word in your language.
☐ Practice reading the words until you can pronounce them correctly.

across	alive	army
behind	between	blew
break	chase	cloud
cross	dead	faithful
middle	path	point
push	serve	shore
sing	thick	trust
wall	watch	wheel

☐ My student can read these words and knows their meanings.   Tutor Initials _____

Lesson 17 – Use Sight & Spelling Words

❑ Read the sentences.   ❑ Draw lines to match the words and pictures.

The fish is jumping to get the bait.

She is serving her favorite kind of pizza.

She's pointing at something with her left hand.

The polar bear has very thick fur.

He is dumping small stones on the path.

The man is watching to see what will happen.

The flag is up, but the mailbox is empty.

That snowman is not alive.

He has two gifts for her; one is behind his back.

She was not afraid, so he kept pushing her.

The phone is between his neck and his shoulder.

His dad is standing behind him
to teach him how to play the game.

She is faithful to visit him and read to him.

❑ My student can read and understand these sentences.   Tutor initials _____

Story 17 ❖ The Red Sea

☐ Read or listen to the story in your native language. Exodus 14:1-31
☐ Find and mark the sight words in the story.   ☐ Listen to the story in English.

across
alive
army
behind
between
blew
break
chase
cloud
cross
dead
faithful
middle
path
point
push
serving
shore
sing
thick
trust
wall
watch
wheel

God led the Israelites out of Egypt in the middle of the night by a pillar of fire. During the day, the fire became a pillar of cloud. God told Moses to have the people camp next to the Red Sea. He said, "I'm going to make Pharaoh stubborn one more time, and he will chase after you."

After the Israelites left, Pharaoh asked, "Why did we let our slaves go? They should be here, serving us." So he took his army and more than 600 fine chariots and chased after them.

The Israelites saw this and cried out to Moses. "Why have you brought us here to die? If we were still serving the Egyptians, they would let us live. But now, because of you, we are all going to die."

Moses told the people, "Don't be afraid! Watch and see what God will do. He will fight for you. Look at the Egyptians. You'll never see them again after today."

The pillar of cloud moved behind the Israelites and came between them and the army that was chasing them. On the Egyptians' side, it was a dark, thick cloud; so they couldn't get close to the Israelites. On the other side, it was a pillar of fire, giving light to God's people.

God said to Moses, "Lift your staff into the air, and point your hand out over the sea. The Israelites are going to the other side – on dry ground."

When Moses pointed his hand to the sea, God caused a strong east wind to push the water back, making a wall on the right side and on the left. All night long, the wind blew on the path between the two walls until the ground was dry. Then Moses told the people to cross over to the other side.

The people went across the sea on dry ground. Pharaoh and his army chased after them on the same path; but when they were in the middle of the sea, their chariot wheels began to break off. Suddenly, the Egyptian army knew they were in trouble. They cried, "Let's get away from the Israelites! The Lord is fighting for them!"

God said to Moses, "Point your hand out over the water." When Moses did that, the sea went back to the way it was before. Water covered the whole Egyptian army; not one of them was left alive! The Israelites saw how the power of God kept them safe as they walked across on dry ground. Yet, water killed the people who were chasing them.

In the morning, there were dead bodies all over the shore. When the Israelites saw the Lord's great power, they put their trust in God and in his faithful servant, Moses. Then they worshiped the Lord with singing.

☐ Read the Story in English.   Tutor initials _____

Review Story 17

☐ Use the words in the boxes to fill in the blanks.

| army | cloud | middle | serving | Watch |

1. God led the Israelites out of Egypt in the _____ of the night by a pillar of fire.
2. During the day, the fire became a pillar of _____.
3. Pharaoh asked, "Why did we let our slaves go? They should be here _____ us."
4. So he took his _____ and more than 600 fine chariots and chased after them.
5. Moses told the people, "Don't be afraid! _____ and see what God will do."

| behind | between | blew | cross | path | point | push | thick | wall |

6. The pillar of cloud moved _____ the Israelites and came _____ them and the army that was chasing them. On the Egyptians' side, it was a dark, _____ cloud; so they couldn't get close to the Israelites. On the other side, it was a pillar of fire, giving light to God's people.
7. God said to Moses, "Lift your staff into the air and _____ your hand out over the sea. The Israelites are going to the other side – on dry ground."
8. When Moses pointed his hand to the sea, God caused a strong east wind to _____ the water back, making a _____ on the right side and on the left.
9. All night long, the wind _____ on the _____ between the two walls, until the ground was dry. Then Moses told the people to _____ over to the other side.

| across | alive | break | chased | dead | faithful | shore | singing | trust | wheels |

10. The people went _____ the sea on dry ground.
11. Pharaoh and his army _____ after them on the same path; but when they were in the middle of the sea, their chariot _____ began to _____ off.
12. Water covered the whole Egyptian army; not one of them was left _____!
13. In the morning, there were _____ bodies all over the _____.
14. When the Israelites saw the Lord's great power, they put their _____ in God and in his _____ servant, Moses. Then they worshiped the Lord with _____.

☐ Read the sentences aloud.   ☐ Tell the story in your own words.   Tutor initials _____

Vocabulary 17 – What are they thinking or saying?

Draw lines to match the words and pictures.

Is that a dead rat over by the wall?

Its a good thing there's nothing breakable in those boxes!

Here, have a pillow behind your head.

I have a gift for you.
And I have one for you, too.

I want my mother.

He went that way.

No, I'm not working. I'm on my break.

I love to watch the raising of the flag.

I felt something in my boot. It's good to dump this water out.

What do you have behind your back?

I find it hard serving this person, but I will be faithful.

I am not happy with the results so far.

Lesson 18

Phonics Word Reading

Words ending with nk ng ing

☐ Practice reading the phonics words until you have mastered them.

Section 1 ~ words ending with nk

rank	crank	tank	thank	bank	blank	blink
ink	pink	wink	link	mink	rink	think
stink	sink	sank	sunk	drink	drank	drunk
bunk	dunk	junk	chunk	trunk	skunk	honk

Section 2 ~ words ending with ng

| bang | fang | gang | hang | rang | sang | lung |
| young | among | long | along | belong | song | strong |

Section 3 ~ words ending with ing

king	ring	bring	sing	sling	blessing	meaning
thing	nothing	being	during	moving	morning	evening
building	having	missing	willing	making	doing	trying
going	giving	living	taking	talking	singing	saying
meeting	getting	looking	coming	working	beginning	ending

☐ My student has mastered the phonics words.   Tutor initials _____

Lesson 18 Spelling (page 1)

Words ending with nk ng ing

☐ Read the word list.   ☐ Read each word again and spell it aloud.

along	among	bank	bring	coming	during
giving	having	king	living	long	making
nothing	taking	thank	thing	think	young

☐ Write the word in your language.   ☐ Draw lines to match the words and sentences.
☐ Use the best English word to fill in the blanks.   ☐ Read the sentences aloud.

along _____   He got a good job working at a _____.

among _____   We can take the kids _____ when we go to the store.

bank _____   My pen was hidden _____ the papers on my desk.

bring _____   My sister is _____ to visit me next month.

coming _____   I made a short phone call _____ my lunch break.

during _____   Will you _____ me a drink of water?

---

giving _____   I was _____ a good time, and I didn't want to leave.

having _____   He was the _____ of a small country in Europe.

king _____   Thank you for _____ me a second chance!

living _____   Some people like _____ in the city.

long _____   They are _____ plans to come here for a visit.

making _____   She came a _____ way to see me.

---

nothing _____   What are you _____ to the potluck?

taking _____   The back door was open, but _____ was taken.

thank _____   There's one _____ I know for sure – God loves you!

thing _____   I want to _____ you for your kindness to me.

think _____   That _____ tree will need plenty of water.

young _____   Do you _____ we have plenty of water for everyone?

☐ Checked by Tutor   Tutor initials _____

Lesson 18 Spelling (page 2)

Words ending with nk ng ing

☐ Read all the words.   ☐ Write the best word under each picture.

| bank | hang | ring | spring | trunk | sing |
| tank | king | sink | building | wing | song |

Spelling Test ☐ Practice the following words until you have learned them.

1. along   4. bring   7. giving   10. living   13. nothing   16. thing
2. among   5. coming   8. having   11. long   14. taking   17. think
3. bank   6. during   9. king   12. making   15. thank   18. young

☐ My student can spell these words aloud.   Tutor Initials _____

☐ My student can write these words when I read them.   Tutor Initials _____

Lesson 18 Sight Words

☐ Write the word in your language.
☐ Practice reading the words until you can pronounce them correctly.

bottom	bread	build
built	camp	fresh
friend	honor	hungry
leader	led	lie
loud	mountain	murder
parent	prophet	shook
sound	steal	taste
third	thirsty	written

☐ My student can read these words and knows their meanings.   Tutor Initials _____

Lesson 18 – Use Sight & Spelling Words

☐ Read the sentences.   ☐ Draw lines to match the words and pictures.

The rings on the logs help us know their age.

I've written a note on the calendar and made a ring around the date.

If you need something, just ring the little bell.

That woman is making fresh bread for her hungry family.

He's having fun making people laugh.

That little house was built near the bottom of two mountains.

He led his horse out of the barn.

Someone left the bottom drawer open.

Our server is bringing a drink on a tray.

She is doing her friend's hair.

They're making plans for building a house.

He's having a rest on the bottom bunk.

That dog has very long ears.

☐ My student can read and understand these sentences.   Tutor initials _____

Story 18 ◆ The Ten Commandments

❏ Read or listen to the story in your native language.

Ex.16:1-15, Ex.19:1-20, Ex.20:1-21, Ex.26:1-6, Deuteronomy 31:1-8, Deut.34:1-10

❏ Find and mark the sight words in the story. ❏ Listen to the story in English.

bottom
bread
build
built
camp
fresh
friend
honor
hungry
leader
led
lie
louder
mountain
murder
parents
prophet
shook
sound
steal
tasted
third
thirsty
written

As Moses led the Israelites in the desert, they became thirsty; so God showed them where they could find water. When the people were hungry, God said, "I will rain down bread from heaven for you." Each morning, the people found fresh food on the ground, and when they tasted it, they called it 'manna'. At times, God sent quail into the camp, so the people had meat to eat.

When they came to Mt. Sinai, they set up camp at the bottom of the mountain. God said to Moses, "I will come down on the mountain and talk to the people."

On the third day, the mountain burned with fire. The ground shook and a cloud covered the whole mountain. There was thunder and lightning.

The people heard what sounded like trumpets that grew louder and louder. Then God said, "I am the Lord your God who brought you out of Egypt."

Moses went up the mountain to talk with God, and he was there for 40 days and 40 nights. God gave Moses two stone tablets with laws written on them. These were God's rules for how people should live their lives.

(1) Do not worship other gods.
(2) Do not make any kind of idol.
(3) Keep God's name holy.
(4) Don't work on the seventh day, but keep it holy.
(5) Honor your parents.
(6) Do not murder.
(7) Do not commit adultery.
(8) Do not steal.
(9) Do not lie to others or about others.
(10) Do not desire to have anything that belongs to someone else.

God also gave Moses plans for how to build the Tabernacle, which was called the House of the Lord. It was a tent that would be put up in the middle of the camp. Because it was a tent, it could be taken down and moved whenever they went to a different place. Workmen built the Tabernacle just the way God said to do it.

When it was time to go into the land of Canaan, Moses told the people that Joshua would be their new leader. Moses said to Joshua, "You will take these people into the land God promised to their forefathers. The Lord will be with you. Therefore, be strong and full of courage!"

Moses died at the age of 120. There was no other prophet as great as Moses – one who talked to God as a person talks with a friend.

❏ Read the Story in English.   Tutor initials _____

Review Story 18

Use the words in the boxes to fill in the blanks.

| bread fresh hungry led tasted thirsty |

1. As Moses _____ the Israelites in the desert, they became _____; so God showed them where they could find water. When the people were _____, God said, "I will rain down _____ from heaven for you."

2. Each morning, the people found _____ food on the ground, and when they _____ it, they called it 'manna'.

| bottom camp louder mountain shook sounded third written |

3. When they came to Mt. Sinai, they set up _____ at the _____ of the mountain.

4. On the _____ day, the mountain burned with fire. The ground _____, and a cloud covered the whole _____. There was thunder and lightning.

5. The people heard what _____ like trumpets that grew _____ and louder. Then God said, "I am the Lord your God who brought you out of Egypt."

6. God gave Moses two stone tablets with laws _____ on them.

| Honor parents murder steal lie friend leader prophet build built |

Some of God's laws: (5) _____ your _____.

(6) Do not _____. (7) Do not commit adultery.

(8) Do not _____. (9) Do not ____ to others or about others.

7. God also gave Moses plans for how to _____ the Tabernacle.

8. Workmen _____ the Tabernacle just the way God said to do it.

9. When it was time to go into the land of Canaan, Moses told the people that Joshua would be their new _____.

10. Moses died at the age of 120. There was no other _____ as great as Moses - one who talked to God as a person talks with a _____.

Read the sentences aloud.   Tell the story in your own words.   Tutor initials _____

Vocabulary 18 ~ What are they thinking or saying?

Draw lines to match the words and pictures.

We can build the new ones right along there next to the ones we built last year.

I have written my letter. Now I will put it in this envelope and mail it.

Mmm! This ice cream tastes so good!

Take this piece of paper and make a written list of what you want.

I don't know if I'm able do that.

That sound is too loud!

This food does not taste good.

I'm making a note of every time you show honor to your leaders.

I'm absolutely positive I can climb to the top of that mountain.

I'm so hungry! This is going to taste good.

I'm coming and bringing this thing to show you what a loud sound it makes.

Of course, I know how to do all those things.

Lesson 19

Phonics Word Reading

Words with th sounds

☐ Practice reading the phonics words until you have mastered them.

Section 1 — words with voiced th

the	this	that	these	those	them	father
there	than	then	they	their	other	mother
brother	rather	gather	smooth	weather	feather	clothing

Section 2 — words with unvoiced th

thin	thick	thing	think	thought	thumb	thunder
thank	thief	thorn	third	thirty	thirsty	Thursday
birthday	method	healthy	nothing	anything	something	everything

Section 3 — words ending with th

bath	math	path	month	birth	death	breath
earth	moth	cloth	broth	with	width	length
north	south	mouth	truth	faith	both	oath
youth	tooth	teeth	worth	growth	health	wealth
fourth	fifth	sixth	seventh	eighth	ninth	tenth

Section 4 — words beginning with thr

| three | throat | throw | threw | thrown | through | throne |
| thrill | thrive | thrift | thrifty | thread | threat | threaten |

☐ My student has mastered the phonics words.   Tutor initials _____

Lesson 19 Spelling (page 1)
Words with th sounds

☐ Read the word list. ☐ Read each word again and spell it aloud.

both	father	mother	month	other	rather
than	that	the	their	them	then
there	these	this	those	three	with

☐ Write the word in your language. ☐ Draw lines to match the words and sentences.
☐ Use the best English word to fill in the blanks. ☐ Read the sentences aloud.

Both _____   My _____ is a kind person like her mom was.
father _____   My _____ is a hard worker like his dad was.
mother _____   _____ of her parents came from Canada.
month _____   My birthday is in the _____ of March.
other _____   Would you _____ live in the country or the city?
rather _____   We always try to help each _____.

than _____   _____ is the man I saw at the store yesterday.
That _____   Tom is much bigger _____ his brother.
the _____   One of _____ best ways to be happy is to help others.
their _____   First we'll eat dinner; _____ we'll have some cake.
then _____   _____ apples are bigger than those in the bag.
These _____   They always wanted _____ own house.

there _____   We gave _____ food and clothes.
them _____   If you need wood, you have to go _____ and get it.
this _____   Mid-afternoon is about _____ o'clock.
with _____   _____ kids are the same ones who came yesterday.
three _____   Last time you made lunch for us; _____ time I'll do it.
Those _____   I will go if you go _____ me.

☐ Checked by Tutor   Tutor initials _____

Lesson 19 Spelling (page 2)

Words with th sounds

☐ Read all the words.　　☐ Write the best word under each picture.

bath	math	mother	three	thumb	thin man
feather	moth	mouth	throne	thorns	teeth

Spelling Test　☐ Practice the following words until you have learned them.

1. both
2. father
3. mother
4. month
5. other
6. rather
7. than
8. that
9. the
10. their
11. them
12. then
13. there
14. these
15. this
16. those
17. three
18. with

☐ My student can spell these words aloud.　Tutor Initials _____

☐ My student can write these words when I read them.　Tutor Initials _____

Lesson 19 Sight Words

❏ Write the word in your language.
❏ Practice reading the words until you can pronounce them correctly.

above	anyone	below
dried	enter	escape
everyone	hurt	kindness
making	maybe	near
our	quickly	roof
soldier	spare	spread
spy	through	tie
tribe	victory	window

❏ My student can read these words and knows their meanings.   Tutor Initials _____

Lesson 19 – Use Sight & Spelling Words

☐ Read the sentences.   ☐ Draw lines to match the words and pictures.

That house has rooms above and below ground level.

The man in the hat is spying on the other person.

He's using a rope to escape through the window.

Three baby ducklings are following their mother.

Both his arm and his neck were hurt.

If he goes quickly, maybe he will get there in time.

He likes to sit and wait with one hand over the other.

She has a walking stick in one hand and a bag in the other.

This is where we enter the city.

They are making plans for better sales next month.

That fruit tree is near the water.

She's holding the gift above her head.

☐ My student can read and understand these sentences.   Tutor initials _____   69

Story 19 ◆ Rahab

☐ Read or listen to the story in your native language. Joshua 2:1-24, Joshua 6:1-27
☐ Find and mark the sight words in the story.   ☐ Listen to the story in English.

above
anyone
below
dried
entered
escape
everyone
hurt
kindness
making
maybe
near
our
quickly
roof
soldier
spare
spread
spy
through
tie
tribe
victory
window

With Joshua as their new leader, the Israelites were making plans to cross over the Jordan River and go into the Promised Land – the land of Canaan. But first, Joshua sent two men to spy out the land. The spies entered into the city of Jericho. It was late in the day, so they found a place to stay at the home of a woman named Rahab.

The king of Jericho found out that the men were there, so he sent soldiers to Rahab's house. They said, "Bring out those men who are here. They are spies."

Rahab had hidden the men under some flax that was spread out on her roof to dry. She told the soldiers, "Those men were here, but they left before the city gate was closed for the night. I don't know which way they went, but if you go quickly, maybe you can find them." So the soldiers went to look for them near the river.

Then Rahab went up on the roof and talked to the two men. "You need to get out of here! But I will help you. I know that God is giving our land to you. All our people are afraid of you. Everyone has heard how the Lord dried up the waters of the Red Sea for you when you left Egypt. Your God is the God of heaven above and of the earth below. I have been kind to you. Please promise me that you will show kindness to my family and spare our lives."

The men said, "If you don't tell anyone about us, we will make sure you are not hurt when the Lord gives us your city." Then they came up with a plan. Rahab's house was on the wall of the city, so she helped the men escape by a rope through the window that night. The men told her, "After we are gone, tie this red rope in your window. Bring all your family into your house and they will be safe. But if anyone leaves your house, they won't be safe."

Rahab told the men, "Hide in the hills for three days. After the soldiers give up looking for you, they will come back to Jericho. Then you can come down from the hills and go back across the river."

The spies did as she said. Then they went back to Joshua and told him everything that had happened. They said, "It's true! God has given us the land. The people are afraid of us."

God gave the Israelites a great victory in taking over the city of Jericho. As soon as they entered the city, the two spies went to Rahab's house and made sure that she and her family were safe. Everyone else in the city was killed.

The Lord was with Joshua, and his fame spread everywhere. Rahab and her family were given a safe place to live near the camp of Israel. In time, she married an Israelite from the tribe of Judah, and they had a son named Boaz.

☐ Read the Story in English.   Tutor initials _____

Review Story 19

☐ Use the words in the boxes to fill in the blanks.

| entered | making | roof | soldiers | spy |

1. The Israelites were _____ plans to cross over the Jordan River and go into the Promised Land – the land of Canaan. But first, Joshua sent two men to _____ out the land.
2. The spies _____ into the city of Jericho. It was late in the day, so they found a place to stay at the home of a woman named Rahab.
3. The king of Jericho found out that the men were there, so he sent _____ to Rahab's house. They said, "Bring out those men who are here. They are spies."
4. Rahab had hidden the men under some flax that was spread out on her _____ to dry.

| above | below | dried | kindness | maybe | near | our | quickly | spare |

5. Rahab told the soldiers, "Those men were here, but they left before the city gate was closed for the night. I don't know which way they went, but if you go _____, _____ you can find them." So the soldiers went to look for them _____ the river.
6. Rahab said, "All _____ people are afraid of you. Everyone has heard how the Lord _____ up the waters of the Red Sea for you when you left Egypt. Your God is the God of heaven _____ and of the earth _____. I have been kind to you. Please promise me that you will show _____ to my family and _____ our lives."

| anyone | escape | everyone | hurt | spread | tie | through | tribe | victory | window |

7. The men said, "If you don't tell _____ about us, we will make sure you are not _____ when the Lord gives us your city."
8. Rahab helped the men _____ by a rope _____ the window that night.
9. The men told her, "After we are gone, _____ this red rope in your _____."
10. God gave the Israelites a great _____ in taking over the city of Jericho.
11. Rahab and her family were safe, but _____ else in the city was killed.
12. The Lord was with Joshua, and his fame _____ everywhere.
13. Rahab married an Israelite from the _____ of Judah, and they had a son named Boaz.

☐ Read the sentences aloud. ☐ Tell the story in your own words. Tutor initials _____

Vocabulary 19 – What are they thinking or saying?

Draw lines to match the words and pictures.

Something's wrong. I don't know if it's diseased or just dried up.

Are you sure you're telling me the truth?

How many more times do we have to go through this practice?

This bath feels so good!

Go away. I don't want to talk to anyone.

Hurrah! We won the victory!

I'm not thin, but I'm not really fat – just a bit thick around the middle.

This way, I can keep my baby near me through the whole day.

We want everyone to come!

This plant dried up while I was away. Someone other than me could have watered it.

All our people welcome you to our country.

There is no job too big for me!

Checked by Tutor   Tutor initials _____

Lesson 20

Phonics Word Reading

Words having the sh sound

☐ Practice reading the phonics words until you have mastered them.

Section 1 – words beginning with sh

she	sheep	sheet	shark	sharp	shoot	shirt
share	shave	shade	shame	shape	shake	shook
shut	shine	shin	shift	shifty	ship	shoes
shack	shed	shield	shop	shot	shock	shocked
show	shown	shelf	shell	shelter	shore	short
should	shook	shadow	shower	shout	shoulder	sheriff

Section 2 – words ending with sh

ash	cash	dash	gash	hash	rash	mash
bush	push	wash	wish	swish	dish	fish
gush	hush	rush	brush	crush	flush	flesh
trash	crash	smash	slash	clash	flash	fresh
punish	finish	foolish	English	Spanish	childish	toothbrush

Section 3 – more words containing sh

fishing   fisherman   washer   dishwasher   flashlight

handshake   mushroom   worship   sunshine   shampoo

shoe polish   push pin   threshing floor

☐ My student has mastered the Phonics Words   Tutor initials _____

Lesson 20 Spelling (page 1)
Words having the sh sound

☐ Read the word list.   ☐ Read each word again and spell it aloud.

cash	finish	fish	fresh	push	rush
shape	share	she	ship	shirt	shoes
shop	shown	shut	trash	wash	wish

☐ Write the word in your language.   ☐ Draw lines to match the words and sentences.
☐ Use the best English word to fill in the blanks.   ☐ Read the sentences aloud.

cash _____   After we _____ our lunch, we will do more work.
finish _____   I need some _____ to buy fruit and bread.
fish _____   You can't pull that door open; you have to _____ it.
fresh _____   Her kitchen always smells like _____ bread.
push _____   She made a cake in the _____ of a heart.
shape _____   Some _____ have all the colors of the rainbow.

ship _____   We need to _____ if we want to get there on time.
rush _____   I have some extra bananas, so I'll _____ with you.
share _____   They will travel by _____ from Alaska to Japan.
She _____   His _____ is a light blue color.
shirt _____   His new _____ are good for walking outdoors.
shoes _____   _____ is one of my favorite people!

shop _____   Please _____ the door when you leave.
shown _____   She is the owner of a small clothing _____.
shut _____   He has _____ me how to use my new phone.
trash _____   I _____ I could go and visit my grandmother.
wash _____   My youngest boy is always happy to take out the _____.
wish _____   It's good to _____ your hands before eating.

☐ Checked by Tutor   Tutor initials _____

Lesson 20 Spelling (page 2)

Words having the sh sound

> ☐ Read all the words.   ☐ Write the best word under each picture.

| shirt | fish | shed | shell | shoe | push pin |
| bush | trash | sheep | ship | shower | shopping |

_____   _____   _____   _____

_____   _____   _____   _____

_____   _____   _____   _____

Spelling Test   ☐ Practice the following words until you have learned them.

1. cash
2. finish
3. fish
4. fresh
5. push
6. rush
7. shape
8. share
9. she
10. ship
11. shirt
12. shoes
13. shop
14. shown
15. shut
16. trash
17. wash
18. wish

☐ My student can spell these words aloud.   Tutor Initials _____

☐ My student can write these words when I read them.   Tutor Initials _____

Lesson 20 Sight Words

☐ Write the word in your language.
☐ Practice reading the words until you can pronounce them correctly.

also	asleep	blessing
chance	doesn't	early
evening	extra	fall
floor	harvest	however
meeting	outside	part
poor	protect	quiet
relative	rich	should
together	tonight	truly

☐ My student can read these words and knows their meanings.   Tutor Initials _____

Lesson 20 – Use Sight & Spelling Words

❑ Read the sentences.   ❑ Draw lines to match the words and pictures.

He is our server, and he also sings.

He's falling asleep in his highchair.

They each have a part in this meeting.

She is cutting paper into animal shapes.

Doing dishes together gives them a chance to talk.

She is sharing with her friends.

The men shown here are relatives.

They are making star-shaped cookies.

She protects her eyes at work.

We had the blessing of an extra good harvest this year.

He's poor, however, she is also poor, so they share.

He is up on his dad's shoulders.

❑ My student can read and understand these sentences.   Tutor initials _____

Story 20 ◆ Ruth

☐ Read or listen to the story in your native language. The Book of Ruth
☐ Find and mark the sight words in the story.   ☐ Listen to the story in English.

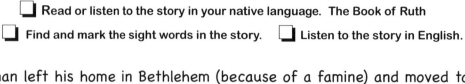

| also |
| asleep |
| blessing |
| chance |
| doesn't |
| early |
| evening |
| extra |
| fall |
| floor |
| harvest |
| however |
| meeting |
| outside |
| part |
| poor |
| protect |
| quietly |
| relative |
| rich |
| should |
| together |
| tonight |
| truly |

A man left his home in Bethlehem (because of a famine) and moved to Moab. He took his wife, Naomi, and their two boys. Not long after, the man died. Their sons grew up and married Moabite women, but then both sons also died. Naomi heard that the famine was over in her home country, so she decided to go back. She told her two daughters-in-law to stay with their families in Moab. But one of them, Ruth, would not leave Naomi; so they went to Bethlehem together.

They were very poor; but it was harvest time, and poor people could 'glean' in the fields. To 'glean' is to pick up grain that falls to the ground during the harvest. So Ruth went to glean in a field owned by a man named Boaz. Late in the day, Boaz saw Ruth and told her, "Don't go to any other field; stay here and work with my servant girls."

Ruth asked, "Why are you so kind to me, a foreigner?"

He said, "We have all heard of your kindness to Naomi, your mother-in-law." Then Boaz went and told his men to let extra grain fall on the ground for Ruth.

That evening, Naomi was happy to hear about the kindness of Boaz. She said, "Oh, Ruth! He's part of our family – a close relative. You should stay in his field."

At the end of the harvest, Naomi said to Ruth, "Tonight, Boaz and his men will sleep outside at the threshing floor in order to protect the grain from being stolen. Go and watch where Boaz lies down. When he is asleep, uncover his feet and lie down. He will tell you what to do.

That night, Ruth went to the threshing floor and waited. When Boaz was asleep, she quietly uncovered his feet and lay down. In the middle of the night, Boaz awoke with a start and saw her at his feet. "Who are you?" he asked.

"I'm Ruth. You are a relative of our family. Spread your protection over me."

Boaz said, "The Lord bless you! You didn't come to our town looking for a husband – rich or poor. Truly, you are a woman of good character! However, there is a next-of-kin who is closer than I am. In the morning, I'll talk to him and give him a chance to redeem you. If he doesn't, then I will do it."

Early the next day, Boaz had a meeting with the other relative and the elders of the town. He said, "Naomi has come back from Moab and is selling her husband's land. You are the closest relative. If you want it, you can buy it. If not, then I will buy it."

The man quickly said. "I'll buy it!"

Boaz said, "However, when you buy it, you must also marry Ruth, the Moabite woman, in order to keep the family name with the land."

The man said, "I can't marry that woman! You may buy the land."

Boaz said, "Then I will buy all of Naomi's land, and I will take Ruth as my wife." To this the elders gave their blessing, and soon Boaz and Ruth were married. They had a son who became the grandfather of David – the great king of Israel. So it was, that Ruth, a Moabite woman, was honored in Israel.

☐ Read the Story in English.   Tutor initials _____

Review Story 20

☐ Use the words in the boxes to fill in the blanks.

| also | extra | falls | harvest | poor | together |

1. Naomi's husband died, and her two sons _____ died.
2. When the famine was over, Ruth and Naomi went to Bethlehem _____ .
3. They were very _____, but it was harvest time, and poor people could glean in the fields.
4. To 'glean' is to pick up grain that _____ to the ground during the _____.
5. Boaz went and told his men to let _____ grain fall on the ground for Ruth.

| asleep | evening | floor | outside | part | protect | quietly | should | Tonight |

6. That _____, Naomi was happy when she heard about the kindness of Boaz.
7. She said, "Oh, Ruth! He's _____ of our family! You _____ stay in his field."
8. At the end of the harvest, Naomi said to Ruth, "_____, Boaz and his men will sleep _____ at the threshing _____ in order to _____ the grain from being stolen. Go and watch where Boaz lies down. When he is _____, uncover his feet and lie down. He will tell you what to do."
9. When Boaz was asleep, Ruth _____ uncovered his feet and lay down.

| blessing | chance | doesn't | Early | However | meeting | relative | rich | Truly |

10. Ruth said, "You are a _____ of our family. Spread your protection over me."
11. Boaz said, "The Lord bless you! You didn't come to our town looking for a husband – _____ or poor. _____, you are a woman of good character!"
12. However, there is a next-of-kin who is closer than I am. In the morning, I'll talk to him and give him a _____ to redeem you. If he _____, then I will do it."
13. _____ the next day, Boaz had a _____ with the other relative. "Naomi is selling her husband's land, and you are the closest relative." The man quickly said, "I'll buy it!"
14. Boaz said, "_____, when you buy it, you must also marry Ruth, the Moabite woman." The man said, "I can't marry that woman! You may buy the land."
15. Boaz said, "Then I will buy all of Naomi's land and I will take Ruth as my wife." To this the elders gave their _____, and soon Boaz and Ruth were married.

☐ Read the sentences aloud.   ☐ Tell the story in your own words.   Tutor initials _____

Vocabulary 20 – What are they thinking or saying?

Draw lines to match the words and pictures.

We had a good meeting. I'm glad
we could finish early.

I like brushing my cat, and I know
he likes it, too.

Do you think I should wear this tonight?

I'll call you back when I finish work.

I feel so tired this morning. Maybe I
got up too early.

I just love working together with you!

I should have been more careful.

I'm just going to drop these into the trash.

I've been wishing for a new hat
and now I have one.

You should take a break more often.
It would do you good.

You're the best grandpa in the world!
I truly love you.

Please protect me!

Certificate of Achievement

My student, _____

has completed all the lessons in

Language Olympics
English Language Learning - Book 2

Congratulations!

Tutor Signature _____

Date _____

Our Mission
Sharing the story of God for discipleship using all the stories of the Bible.

Our Websites
BibleTelling.org – all BibleTelling news, events, and services (including Seminars in Israel, Training, and free download of All the Stories of the Bible)
BTStories.com – free online access to audio, video, text, timeline, map, and insights for *All the Stories of the Bible*
ChristianStorytelling.com – official website of the annual conference
LanguageOlympics.org – literacy and ESL training using 60 Bible stories

Our Media and Resources
YouTube video series: https://bit.ly/2rLOZFY – The Art of Storytelling
Amazon books/ebooks: https://amzn.to/2j7LER2 – Author page for John Walsh
Amazon books/ebooks: https://amzn.to/2Tpzcup – Author page for Jan Walsh

Story of the Day Subscription
Receive an e-mail each weekday with links to the video, audio, and narrative of the story of the day.
E-mail your subscription request to **info@BibleTelling.com**.

Facebook
Search for "BibleTelling"

Mobile App
Search for "BT Stories" in the Apple, Android, and Windows app stores

Contact
E-mail us at info@BibleTelling.com with any questions.

Post comments or questions on our Facebook page.

BibleTelling
2905 Gill Street
Bloomington, IL 61704

Made in the USA
Middletown, DE
07 March 2023

26362060R10049